GREAT CONTROL OVER YOUR EMOTIONS

STASIA ANNE

Table of Contents

INTRODUCTION

Definition of Emotion

It is a conscious mental reaction (such as anger or fear) subjectively experienced as strong feeling usually directed toward a specific object and typically accompanied by physiological and behavioural changes in the body. It can also be seen as the affective aspect of consciousness or feeling.

 Emotional health on the other hand is about **how we think and feel**. It is about our sense of wellbeing, our ability to cope with life events and how we acknowledge our own emotions as well as those of others.

There are times our emotions get out of our control. There are processes to be able to have control over our emotions and manage them. We are going to talk about these processes.

CHAPTER ONE

EMOTION RECOGNITION

Please understand if you are not feeling great. Emotion recognition is the process of recognizing and acknowledging your own emotions. Being aware of your emotions can help you better manage and improve your mental health. When a person feels a certain emotion, there is usually an accompanying physical or mental reaction. By paying attention to your own physical and mental cues, you can identify when you are experiencing certain emotions. For example, you are sitting in a restaurant. A friend meets you for lunch. She is already ten minutes late. "Well, she's keeping me waiting," you think, then you find yourself repeatedly tapping a water glass with a straw. Both the resulting thoughts and the resulting actions help you recognize that you are feeling impatient.

Observe your thoughts and actions for a day or two. How do they alert you to your emotional state? Record these observations in your journal as a first step toward greater emotional awareness.

CHAPTER TWO

NOTICE WHEN YOUR EMOTIONS ARE PULLING AWAY FROM YOU

Be careful when you feel your emotions pulling away from you. The first step in getting your emotions under control is recognizing that they are out of control. Ask yourself how it feels physically and mentally and work on identifying it in the moment. requires rational thinking. Only awareness anchors you in the present moment

Take a deep breath to calm yourself down. When your emotions separate you, your breathing becomes uncontrollable, and stress and anxiety increase. Take a few deep breaths and calm your mind and body to break this spiral. If possible, try targeted deep breathing for the most effective solution

You could also make notes of your emotions, when you feel them, what causes them and what stops them. This gives you a better insight of your emotions and it makes it easier to handle.

CHAPTER THREE

ALLOW YOURSELF TO FEEL YOUR EMOTIONS

Feel your emotions. When people are sad, angry, anxious, embarrassed, or otherwise distressed, they often do things to make them feel better. This may be a natural reaction, but it's important to feel emotions as they arise rather than trying to change them. Take time to recognize your emotions and stay with your emotions. It can be uncomfortable, but it's an important step in dealing with it. Do not judge yourself or your emotions. Just feel them, accept them, and let them pass you by. That doesn't mean you should be worried or overwhelmed for days. Seek help from a therapist if you feel this way and are unable to let go or process your emotions.

CHAPTER FOUR

EXPRESS YOUR EMOTIONS IN A HEALTHY MANNER

Express your feelings in a healthy way. Once you learn to recognize the mental and physical signals of your emotions, you can find positive ways to express them. Emotional expression is necessary because suppressing or repressing emotions can lead to unhealthy outcomes such as depression and anxiety. There are many ways to express your feelings in a constructive and helpful way. Losing emotional control often results in a loss of self and space. You get carried away by your emotions and you don't know where you are. To combat this, focus your attention on what is around you and on the physical sensations you are experiencing.

Relaxes muscles and relieves physical and mental tension. Do a body scan to see where the stress is and force that area to relax. Keep your hands off, your shoulders relaxed and your legs relaxed. Rotate your head and wave your fingers. Relieving tension in your body can go a long way toward calming your mind. Imagine yourself in a quiet and safe place.

Choose a real or imaginary place where you feel calm and relaxed. Close your eyes, imagine, breathe slowly and evenly, and create as much detail as possible. Relieves tension in the body and allows the tranquillity of a safe space to soothe thoughts and emotions

CHAPTER FIVE

EMOTION MANAGEMENT

Talking to others is one of his best ways to express his feelings. Just make sure the person you're sharing with supports you and doesn't criticize you. Think of a best friend, sibling, or counsellor.

Writing your feelings also helps. Write your thoughts in a diary. Over time, you can look back at these entries and see if patterns emerge. Of course journaling is good for mental health. Especially if you use it to solve problems, not just diverge.

Cry when necessary. When people are sad, they may suppress their feelings out of guilt or shame. Also, sometimes I can't cry even when I'm sad. Watching movies, reading literature, and listening to music can help you talk about your emotional state and shed tears.

Relieve tension. Anger is one of the most difficult emotions to express. Because what you do when you're angry can be socially unacceptable. For example, yelling at someone you love, breaking things, or banging on walls may not be a good idea. Instead, you can use some of the same stress management techniques to help you overcome your anger—try exercising vigorously or shouting into your pillow.

CHAPTER SIX

CAREFULLY EXPRESSING YOURSELF

Be careful how you express your feelings to others. If you are upset while talking to someone, pause and return to the conversation when you are able to express yourself properly. Use "I feel" statements to manage anger and other emotions and avoid blame. For example, instead of saying, "I feel hurt and angry when you talk to me like this," say, "You make me very angry." You should also make sure to calmly talk to the person and then take a few deep breaths when you feel like you would implode with rage. If you talk to someone or express yourself when angry you could increase your anger and you might not solve the situation.

If you want to talk to someone who upset you, do not do it in a fit of rage because you might go about it the wrong way and possibly regret it when you are calm. Any action or word you say when angry might become worse than what initially caused the anger.

CHAPTER SEVEN

ALL EMOTIONS ARE ESSENTIAL

Both negative and positive emotions are essential. Please understand that People like to express their joy, excitement and love. But pushing negative emotions away seems to be the right thing to do. You may have grown up thinking it was taboo to show anger, shame, or frustration, so you repress those feelings. In fact, feelings only get worse. Repressed emotions can contribute to mental illnesses such as anxiety and depression.

Resist the temptation to hide or suppress your negative emotions. Negative emotions such as sadness and anger are just as important for mental health as positive emotions. These emotions give us insight into what is important to us and what we need to change about ourselves and the people around us. So be careful to put everything outside instead of keeping it inside.

CHAPTER EIGHT

GIVE YOURSELF FREEDOM

Detachment from intense emotions can help you respond appropriately. This distance can be physical, such as moving away from a stressful situation. But distractions can also create mental distance. You don't want to block or avoid your emotions entirely, but distractions don't hurt until you're in the right place to deal with them. Be sure to get back to them. Healthy distractions are temporary.

Trials: walks, watch funny videos, talk to loved ones, spend a few minutes with your pet.

TRY TO MEDITATE

If you already practice meditation, this might be one of his favorite ways to deal with extreme emotions. Meditation helps you become more aware of all your emotions and experiences. When you meditate, you teach yourself to sit with those feelings. As mentioned earlier, it becomes easier to regulate your emotions when you learn to accept all of your emotions. Meditation helps improve these receptive skills. It also offers other benefits. B. Relax and sleep better

CHAPTER NINE

CONTROL STRESS

Being under a lot of stress can make it difficult to deal with your emotions. Even people who are usually good at controlling their emotions can struggle during times of tension and stress. Reducing stress or finding more helpful ways to deal with stress can help you better control your emotions. Mindfulness practices such as meditation can also help reduce stress. You can't get rid of it, but they can make living with it easier. Other healthy ways to deal with stress include: getting enough sleep Take time to talk (and laugh) with your friends, exercise, spend time in nature, recreation and hobby time.

CHAPTER TEN

UNDERSTANDING YOUR EMOTIONS

When you understand yourself and your emotions you would know how to avoid certain emotions not needed and how to manage it. You could also identify what works better for you and what doesn't . Proper management of your emotions would help you a lot in your daily activities and relationships.